WRITING
ABOUT MOVIES

Karen M. Gocsik

Dartmouth College

Richard M. Barsam

Emeritus, Hunter College

W. W. NORTON & COMPANY

NEW YORK LONDON

Copyright © 2007 by W. W. Norton & Company, Inc.

Composition by GGS Information Services, Inc.
Manufacturing by VonHoffmann, Inc.
Book design by Lissi Sigillo.
Production manager: Benjamin Reynolds.

Library of Congress Cataloging-in-Publication Data
Gocsik, Karen M.
  Writing about movies / Karen M. Gocsik, Richard Barsam.
     p. cm.

ISBN-13: 978-0-393-92983-6 (pbk.)
ISBN-10: 0-393-92983-3 (pbk.)

  1. Film criticism. I. Barsam, Richard Meran. II. Title.

PN1995.G547 2006
808'.066791—dc22

                                                          2006046617

W. W. Norton & Company, Inc., 500 Fifth Avenue, New York, N. Y. 10110
www.wwnorton.com

W. W. Norton & Company Ltd., Castle House, 75/76 Wells Street, London WIT 3QT

3 4 5 6 7 8 9 0

Contents

The Challenges of Writing About Movies

What's so hard about writing about movies? After all, we all "know" movies. Most of us could recite the plot of *Independence Day* more easily than we could recite the Declaration of Independence. We know more about the characters who perished on Cameron's *Titanic* than we know about many of the people who inhabit our own lives.

It's precisely our familiarity with film, however, that presents our greatest writing challenge. Film is so familiar and so prevalent in our lives that we are often lulled into passive viewing (at worst) or simple entertainment (at best). As a result, certain aspects of a film are often "invisible." Caught up in the entertainment, we sometimes don't "see" the camera work, composition, editing, or lighting. Nor do we "hear" the sound design. Nor do we observe the production struggles that accompany every film—including the script's many rewrites, the drama of getting the project financed, the casting challenges, and so on.

However, when your film professor asks you to write about film, it's precisely those "invisible" aspects that you're expected to see. As *Looking at Movies* advises, you need to pay attention to the way the camera moves. Observe the composition (the light, shadow, and arrangement) within the frame. Think about how the film was edited. Note the sound design. In short, consider the elements that make up the film. How do they function, separately and together? Also think about the film in the context of when it was made, how, and by whom. In breaking down the film into its constituent parts, you'll be able to *analyze* what you see. In short, you'll be able to write a paper that transforms your thoughts and responses into writing that is appropriately academic.

What Is Academic Writing?

Simply put, *academic writing* is writing done by scholars for other scholars—and that includes you. As a college student, you are engaged in activities that scholars have been engaged in for centuries: you will read about, think about, argue about, and write about great ideas. Of course, being a scholar requires that you read, think, argue, and write in certain ways. You will need to make and support your claims according to the expectations of the academic community.

How do you determine what these expectations are? It might help to think about scholarship as if it were an ongoing dinner party to which you have been recently invited. The conversation (which in this case is about movies) has been going on for quite a while when you arrive. What do you do? Do you sit down and immediately voice your opinion? Or do you listen, try to gauge the lay of the land, determine what contribution you might make, and then make it?

The etiquette that you would employ at the dinner party is precisely the strategy that you should use when you write academic papers. In short, listen to what other scholars are saying. Familiarize yourself with the scholarly conversation before jumping in. Books like *Looking at Movies* are the perfect "dinner companion" for film scholarship, getting you up to speed, filling you in on the conversation that preceded you. But you should make use of other resources too. Your professor, for instance, is a living, breathing expert on what film scholars care about. Books, journals, and even credible Internet sites also offer an opportunity to eavesdrop on the ongoing scholarly conversation about film. Once you understand the conversation, you can begin to construct an informed argument of your own.

Constructing an Informed Argument

Consider What You Know When you sit down to write an academic paper, you'll first want to consider what you know about your topic. Different writing assignments require different degrees of knowledge. A short paper written in response to a viewing of Alfred Hitchcock's *Rear Window*, for example, may not require you to be familiar with Hitchcock's other films.

However, if you're asked to write an academic paper on the film, you'll want to know more. You'll want to have a firm grasp of the terms covered in *Looking at Movies* so that you can explain how Hitchcock is building his film. You'll want to be familiar with Hitchcock's other films so that you can understand what themes are important to Hitchcock and his work. Finally, if you're watching this film in an upper-level film class, you'll want to be aware of different critical perspectives on Hitchcock's films and on films in general, so that you can "place" your argument within the ongoing critical conversation.

Consider What You Think The aim in thinking about your topic is to come up with a fresh observation. After all, it's not enough to summarize in a paper what's already known and discussed. You must also add something of your own to the conversation.

Understand, however, that "adding something of your own" is not an invitation to bring your own personal associations, reactions, or experiences to the reading of a film. To create an informed argument, you must first recognize that your writing should be *analytical* rather than personal. In other words, your writing must show that your associations, reactions, and experiences of a film have been framed in a critical, rather than a personal, way.

This is not to say that your personal responses to a film are irrelevant. Indeed, your personal responses are a good starting point for the academic work to come. For instance, being terrified when you watch *The Blair Witch Project* can be the first step on the way to a strong analysis. Interrogate your terror. Why are you scared? What elements of the film contribute to your terror? How does the film play with the horror and documentary genres in order to evoke a fear that is fresh and convincing?

Interrogating your personal responses is the first step in making sure that your argument will be appropriately academic. To help ensure that your responses are critical rather than personal, subject them to the following critical thinking processes: summary, evaluation, analysis, and synthesis.

Summarize The first step in thinking critically about film is to summarize what the film is saying. You can construct several different summaries, depending on your agenda. But beware: even the most basic of summaries—the plot summary—isn't as simple as it seems. It's difficult to write both economically and descriptively, to discern what's essential to your discussion and what's not.

Consider this: Orson Welles's *Citizen Kane* has a very complex plot using seven narrators and consisting of nine parts (five of which include flashback sequences). Further complicating matters is that the story duration is about seventy years, while the plot duration is one week of a reporter's research. *Citizen Kane* is a notoriously difficult film to sum up—though the following plot summary by Jesse Garon, taken from the Internet Movie Database (IMDb), does an excellent job:

> Multimillionaire newspaper tycoon Charles Foster Kane dies alone in his extravagant mansion, Xanadu, speaking a single word: "Rosebud." In an attempt to figure out the meaning of this word, a reporter tracks down the people who worked and lived with Kane; they tell their stories in a series of flashbacks that reveal much about Kane's life but not enough to unlock the riddle of his dying breath.

What makes this summary effective? It follows the basic structure of any film: a conflict/riddle/problem is proposed; someone tries to solve the problem, meeting obstacles along the way; finally, the problem is resolved. The writer of this summary traces the conflict without being sidetracked by the many plot complications. He sticks to the theme and to the basic conflict/resolution structure. He also makes sure that his sentences are simple and clear. In the end, he produces a summary that is faithful to the film but that doesn't overwhelm the reader with details.

Summarizing a film's plot helps you to see its structure, conflicts, and themes. But when thinking critically about a film, you needn't limit yourself to plot summary. Equally useful, depending on your purpose, are summaries of a film's production values (lighting, editing, sound), its production history (financing, casting, distribution), or its critical reception (reviews, scholarship, and so on). The point is that summarizing is useful in helping you clarify what you know about a film, laying the foundation for the more complex processes to come.

Evaluate Evaluation is an ongoing process. You evaluate a film the moment you encounter it, and—if you aren't lazy—you continue to evaluate and to reevaluate as you go along. As we've been saying, evaluating a film is different from reacting to a film. When you evaluate for an academic purpose, you need to clearly articulate and support your own personal response. What in the film is leading you to respond a certain way? What's *not* in the film that might be contributing to your response? Watching *Citizen Kane*, for instance, you are likely to have found yourself caught up in the film's suspense. What in the film is making you feel this way? The editing? The acting? The script? Can you point to a moment in the film that is particularly successful in creating suspense? In asking these questions, you are straddling two intellectual processes: experiencing your own personal response, and analyzing the film.

Evaluation also encourages you to compare a film with other films that you've seen. How does the acting in *Citizen Kane* compare with the acting in other films from the same era? What about the editing? The camera angles? The sound? The story? How do they compare? Evaluating what's special about a film allows you to isolate those aspects that are most interesting—and most fruitful—to investigate further.

Analyze In the analysis stage of constructing an informed argument, your first task is to consider the parts of your topic that most interest you, then examine how these parts relate to each other or to the whole. To analyze *Citizen Kane*, you will want to break the film down by examining particular scenes, point of view, camera movements, sound, and so on. In short, you'll want to ask, What are the components of Welles's film, and how do these components contribute to the film's theme? How do they contribute to Welles's work as a whole? When you analyze, you break the whole into parts so that you might see the whole differently. When you analyze, you find things to say.

Helping students to analyze movies by isolating their parts (shots, editing, sound, lighting, and so on) and determining their relationship to the whole is the purpose of *Looking at Movies*. We'll discuss the matter of analyzing films at length later in this supplement.

Synthesize When you analyze, you break down a film into its parts. When you synthesize, you look for *connections* between ideas. Consider once again *Citizen Kane*. In analyzing this film, you might come up with elements that seem initially disparate. You might have some observations that at first don't seem to gel. Or you might have read various critical perspectives on the film, all of them in disagreement with one another. Now would be the time to consider whether these disparate elements or observations might be reconciled, or synthesized. This intellectual exercise requires that you create an *umbrella argument*—a larger argument under which several observations and perspectives might stand.

For example, consider the analysis of *Citizen Kane* in *Looking at Movies* (pages 278–282). The author observes a series of elements that initially seem at odds with one another. For instance, he notes the range of conflicting emotions that the actors experience (each shifts among various feelings that include tenderness, joy, annoyance, guilt, and rage). He notes, too, how the interior and exterior actions contradict our typical expectations (whereas outside in the snow the boy Charles plays gleefully, inside the house, which one would expect to be warmer, the lamps remain unlit and the action is cold and strained). The point that the author makes by calling our attention to these conflicting aspects of the film is that Welles is constructing a scene rich in ambiguity. The effect, the author argues, is that Welles, through this ambiguity, is shifting the challenge of interpreting the scene to the viewer. This idea synthesizes the author's many observations, transforming a list of points into a powerful and intriguing argument.

Finding a Rhetorical Stance

When writing an academic paper, you must consider not only what you want to say, but also the audience to whom you're saying it. In other words, it's important to determine not only what *you* think about a topic, but also what your audience is likely to think. What biases does your audience have? Values? Expectations? Knowledge? To whom are you writing, and for what purpose?

When you begin to answer all of these questions, you have started to reckon with what has been called the rhetorical stance. *Rhetorical stance* refers to the position you take as a writer in terms of the subject and the reader of your paper.

Consider Your Position Let's first consider your relationship to the topic you're writing about. When you write a paper, you take a stand on a topic. You determine whether you're for or against it, passionate or cool-headed. You determine whether you'll view this topic through a particular perspective (e.g., feminist), or whether you'll make a more general response.

To ensure that your stance on a topic is appropriately analytical, you might want to ask yourself some questions. Begin by asking why you've taken this particular stance. For instance, why did you find some elements of the film more important than others? Does this prioritizing reflect a bias or preconception on your part? If you dismissed part of the film as boring or unimportant, why? Do you have personal issues or experiences that lead you to be impatient with certain elements? Might any part of your response to the film cause readers to discount your paper as biased or uncritical? If so, you might want to reconsider your position.

Consider Your Audience Your position on a topic does not, by itself, determine your rhetorical stance. You must also consider your readers. In the college classroom, the audience is usually the professor or your classmates—although occasionally your professor will instruct you to write for a more particular or more general audience. No matter who your readers are, you'll want to consider them carefully before you start to write.

What do you know about your readers and their stance toward your topic? What are they likely to know about the topic? What biases are they likely to have? Moreover, what effect do you hope to have on the readers? Is your aim to be controversial? Informative? Entertaining? Will the readers appreciate or resent your intention?

Once you've determined who your readers are, you will want to consider how you might best reach them. If, for example, you're an authority on a subject and you're writing to readers who know little or nothing about the subject, you'll want to take an informative stance. If you aren't yet confident about a topic and you have more questions than answers, you might want to take an inquisitive stance.

In any case, when you're deciding on a rhetorical stance, choose one that allows you to be sincere. You don't want to take an authoritative stance on a subject if you aren't confident about what you're saying. On the other hand, you don't want to avoid taking a position on a subject; nothing is worse than reading a paper in which the writer has refused to take a stance. What if you are of two minds on a subject? Declare that to the reader. Make ambivalence your clear rhetorical stance.

Finally, don't write simply to please your professor. Though some professors find it flattering to discover that all of their students share their positions on a subject, most of us are hoping that your argument will engage us by telling us something new about your topic—even if that "something new" is simply a fresh emphasis on a minor detail. Moreover, it's impossible for you to replicate the "ideal paper" that exists in your professor's head. When you try, you risk having your analysis compared to your professor's. Is that really what you want?

Using Appropriate Tone and Style

You understand what's required of you in an academic paper. You need to be analytical. Critical. You need to create an informed argument. You need to consider your relationship to the topic and to the reader. But what about finding an appropriate academic tone and style?

One thing to remember as you analyze and write about film is that you aren't writing a review. Reviews are generally subjective: they explore an individual's response to a film and thus do not require research or analysis. As a result, reviews are often both simplistic (thumbs up, thumbs down) and "clever" (employing the pun-driven or sensational turns of phrase of popular magazines). Although reviews can be useful and even entertaining pieces of prose, they generally don't qualify as "academic writing."

The tone and style of academic writing might at first seem intimidating. But that needn't be the case. Professors want students to write clearly and intelligently on matters that they, the students, care about. What professors *don't* want is imitation scholarship—that is, exalted gibberish that no one cares to read. If the student didn't care to write the paper, the professor probably won't care to read it. The tone of an academic paper, then, must be inviting to the reader, even while it maintains an appropriate academic style.

Remember that professors are human beings, capable of boredom, laughter, irritation, and awe. Understand that you're writing to a person who will be delighted when you make your point clearly, concisely, and persuasively. Understand, too, that she will be less delighted if you have inflated your prose, pumped up your page count, or tried to impress her by using terms that you didn't take the time to understand. (For more on how to create an appropriate but engaging academic tone and style, see "Attending to Style" later in this supplement.)

Kinds of Film Papers

Now that you have a sense of what it means to write an academic paper, you can think about what you need to do to write successfully about film. Film studies is a broad and fascinating field. Scholars who write in this discipline write not only about particular films, but also about the filmmakers, industry, cultures, and histories that make these films. Let's turn our attention now to some of the kinds of papers that you will be asked to write in a film studies course.

Formal Analysis

Formal analysis of a film or films requires the viewer to break down the film into its component parts and discuss how those parts contribute to the whole. Formal analysis can be understood as taking apart a tractor in a field: you lay out the parts, try to understand the function and purpose of each one, and then put the parts back together so that the tractor runs better than it did before.

The most typical writing assignment in an introductory film studies course looks at how a single cinematic element functions in a single film. Although some instructors provide detailed instructions in their assignments—which topic to cover, which elements to discuss, possibly even which scene or shot to analyze—others permit students to choose the movie and the overall topic they wish to discuss. Thus, you might write a paper about discontinuity editing in *Black Hawk Down*, or the use of the Steadicam in *The Motorcycle Diaries*, or the use of sound in *A Man Escaped*. Each of these topics clearly focuses on describing the use and interpreting the effectiveness of a single cinematic element in a single movie.

Sometimes a professor will ask you to do a formal analysis paper comparing and/or contrasting two or more films. The following titles show how the comparative approach is well suited to forceful, interesting papers:

1. "Domestic Ideals and Film Noir Dysfunction in Ridley Scott's *Blade Runner* (1982) and Frank Capra's *It's a Wonderful Life* (1946)"
2. "Horror Film Violence Before and After Alfred Hitchcock's *Psycho* (1960)"
3. "French and American Style and Sensibility in Luc Besson's *Nikita* (1990) and John Badham's *Point of No Return* (1993)"

The first example promises to compare ideology and genre across two seemingly diverse films, both of which include film noir elements. The second example makes a historical contrast, a before-and-after argument. The third example compares national cinemas as it considers the same story told in two different countries: *Nikita* in France and *Point of No Return*, the remake, in the United States.

The compare/contrast format works very well if you take two things assumed to be very similar and show important differences (say, contrasting *The Godfather* with *The Godfather: Part II*), or if you take two things assumed to be very dissimilar and show important similarities (as in the suggested comparison between *Blade Runner* and *It's a Wonderful Life*). But for a compare/contrast paper to be effective, the writer must be sure to limit the comparison to the most salient points. A paper that articulates carefully a few important comparisons and/or contrasts and analyzes their significance will fare much better than a paper that simply presents a laundry list of similarities and differences with no analysis or commentary.

Film History

All films are deeply involved in history: they reflect history, influence history, *have* history. A film like *Gone With the Wind* not only tells a story of the South during the Civil War, but (more importantly) it reflects the values and ideas of the culture that produced it, and so it can be understood as a historical document.

All films are part of our culture's history. They derive from and contribute to historical events. War films, for example, take their substance from historical events. They also influence those events—by inspiring wartime audiences to rally behind the troops, or to protest them.

Films also have their own histories:

> All films have production histories, which involve the details of how and why and when they were made. Production problems often (if not always) affect what we see on the screen.
> All films have distribution and release histories: some films are released to different generations of audiences, to wildly different responses; other films are banned because they threaten certain cultural values. (Thailand, for example, banned both *The King and I* and the more recent *Anna and the King* because, in the estimation of the Thais, the films were disrespectful to their royalty).
> All films have economic and industrial histories. Hollywood films are vulnerable to certain economic and industrial pressures; China's cinema and India's Bollywood have their own economic and industrial histories that influence the films that they produce.

> All films have an audience. Some have a fan base. The history of these communities—and their reactions to films—offers an interesting view into how a public influences what films are produced, how they're shot and edited, how they're distributed, and so on.

> Finally, all films should be understood in the larger context of film history. A particular film might "make" history through its technological innovations, or it might reflect certain historical trends.

Ideological Papers

Even films that are made to entertain promote a set of beliefs. Sometimes these beliefs are clearly political, even propagandistic: Eisenstein's *Battleship Potemkin*, for example, is a glorification of Soviet values. Other films are not overtly political, but they still promote certain values; *Mary Poppins*, for example, argues for the idea that fathers need to take a more active interest in their families.

When watching a film, it's important to remember that even films whose purpose it is to entertain may be promoting or even manipulating our feelings about a certain set of values. *Independence Day*, for example, is entertaining, in part, because it plays on our feelings of American superiority and "never say die." An analysis of the film benefits from a consideration of these values, and how they're presented in the film.

Finally, students familiar with different schools of criticism—Marxism, feminism, new historicism, and any of the other isms—can use these critical frameworks to come up with ideas for writing. For instance, if you want to write a paper on Jane Campion's *The Piano* (1993), you can view the film through a Marxist lens, exploring it in economic terms, focusing on matters of privilege and power. Or you can take a feminist perspective, considering how the heroine's cultural situation (or Campion's) is relevant to the themes of the film.

Cultural Studies/National Cinemas

Films reflect the cultures and nations in which they were produced. Hollywood films, one might argue, reflect certain things about our nation's culture: our love of distraction, our attraction to adrenaline and testosterone, our need for good to triumph over evil, and our desire for things work to out in the end.

Other cultures and nations have different values and thus produce different sorts of films. Sometimes these films baffle us. We might watch a French film, for example, and wonder why it's funny. Or we might watch a Russian film and wonder why the director never calls for a close-up. These observations are, in fact, excellent starting places. Consider differences. Find out if these differences reflect something about the national character, or if they reflect trends in the national cinema. You may find that you have something interesting to say.

Auteur Criticism

Auteur criticism understands a film as the product of a single person and his vision. In most cases, this person is the director. Auteur criticism is useful because it helps us to understand, for example, what makes a certain film a "Spielberg" film. However, auteur criticism is sometimes based on the erroneous assumption that films are like novels—that is, that *one* person is the author.

The idea of the author's presence in a cinematic work has been long debated. Whereas some critics argue that a work's coherence depends on the vision and decisions of a single person, critics in the opposing camp believe that it's the structure of a work—and not the personality that created it—that we can justly address.

Complicating the matter further is that film is a collaborative medium. It's important to understand that no one person can control the product. The director of photography, the screenwriters (often many), the wardrobe and makeup people, the head of the studio—all these and others have a hand in determining the final product of a film.

Still, auteur criticism is widely practiced and is useful in helping us to understand the common themes and aesthetic decisions in films by the same director (or producer, or star). Keep in mind, however, that the best of the auteur criticism draws on other sources, like film history or formal analysis, to ensure that the paper is not simply an examination of the private life or the psychology of the auteur.

The Process of Writing About Movies

In some ways, writing about movies is similar to writing on any subject: you must choose a topic, generate ideas, craft a thesis, research and structure your argument, and find the proper tone. But each of these more general tasks requires you to perform some tasks that are specific to film studies. For instance, you must know how to view films, how to annotate shot sequences, how to use film-specific language, and how to search film-specific databases. The following section combines general and film-specific writing advice with the aim of helping you produce better papers for your film studies classes.

Choosing a Topic

In a typical film studies assignment, you will generally have two important choices to make: (1) what movie do you want to discuss, and (2) what elements of that movie are most compelling—design, acting, editing, lighting, camera work, sound? Often you'll want to discuss several films; when you do, selecting the element that most interests you can help you narrow your topic.

For instance, if you want to write about editing that creates mood, ask the following questions about each film on your short list: What sorts of editing does this film employ? What moods does the editing help create? Which movie's editing most strongly holds your interest? Why? Does that editing reflect a clear system of expression? Can it provide a sufficient number of good examples both to sustain your interest *and* to support your thesis? Will you be enthusiastic enough about the movie to view it several times so that you can fully grasp how the director uses editing to develop mood?

Viewing Films

Once you've chosen a film, you'll want to watch it as many times as necessary to find the appropriate examples to support your analysis. The next step is to choose which format you're going to use (DVD, videotape, or Internet).

The Advantages of DVDs In studying the movie you're going to write about, you will most likely use a copy on videotape (VHS) or digital video disc (DVD). Each provides convenient playback options for students of film, but the DVD is standard for its flexibility and practicality in helping you take notes.

On DVD playback systems, the ability to freeze single frames and to play a shot back at a fraction of the original speed allows you to carefully study the composition and choreography of a shot, or to view details of setting and background. It also offers you the option to jump forward and backward between scenes, as well as a timer for noting the exact location of a shot or scene. Because sound and image are so carefully integrated and so compelling together, you might watch a scene with the sound off, or turn your back to the screen and listen to a film. The fast-forward and rewind functions might even reveal something about plotting and structure impossible to notice at regular speed, such as the repetition of cinematic elements, motifs, or themes.

One additional advantage of DVDs (particularly those marked "collector's edition") is that they contain features about the making of the movie—interviews with key creative personnel, commentary by film scholars, and even deleted footage. These extras offer students of film an unprecedented wealth of material once reserved for industry insiders or academics lucky enough to visit studios, film libraries, and special collections. Indeed, the extras are often as interesting, if not as charming, as the movies themselves.

For instance, the DVD for Cameron Crowe's *Almost Famous* includes all of Crowe's *Rolling Stone* articles, which were the original inspiration for the film. These articles provide a convenient means of tracing the ways in which Crowe's semi-autobiographical film combines, elaborates on, and distorts parts of his background as a teenage rock-and-roll journalist. A director's edition DVD, *Untitled: Almost Famous the Bootleg Cut*, provides even more extra materials, including thirty-six minutes of previously unseen footage. Such unused or deleted scenes and shots provide interesting lessons in the decision-making process of filmmakers.

Because many deleted scenes were dropped before they underwent sound editing, effects work, and color correction (that is, they are "rough cuts"), these extras can provide dramatic lessons in the degree to which Hollywood polishes its final product—a reminder that the "realism" and naturalness of the final release is a carefully shaped and crafted construction. For instance, the bonus footage of Frank Oz's heist film *The Score* includes three takes of a scene in which Max (Marlon Brando) tries to persuade his longtime accomplice in crime, Nick (Robert De Niro), to commit to a new heist. Oz uses the common shot/reverse shot, an over-the-shoulder treatment. The three takes we see outside the context of the film focus on Brando and vividly illustrate his improvisational talents. Viewing these takes in relation to the final scene in the film makes clear how Oz and his editor, Richard Pearson, have combined the best bits of multiple takes into a seamless whole.

Taking Notes As you watch films for class, carefully note your observations, reactions, and insights. There are no rules for note taking because it's a highly personal activity, but here are several useful hints:

> Don't take your eyes off the screen while you're jotting down notes about what you see. Something very important can occur in the time it takes to shift your eyes from the screen to your notes and then back to the screen.
> Make your notes as succinct as possible.
> Resist the temptation to record all of your observations. Focus instead on the items that relate to your paper.
> Make rough sketches of shots that you want to discuss. These will prove very useful when you begin to write. You can also use an inexpensive software program (such as Snapz Pro X for Macs) to grab images from a DVD and insert them into your paper as illustrations.

> Use the conventional shorthand for describing types of shots (e.g., *CU* for *close-up*). This shorthand will not only speed up the process but will get you in the habit of using film terms.

> Make note of the timing of each shot that you want to discuss—for instance, 09:43—so that you can easily find it again if you need to.

> Review and organize your notes according to any patterns or categories that may appear. Do this while the viewing is still fresh in your mind. Many students come up with ideas for their papers when they reorganize the observations in their notes.

Annotating Shot Sequences With the goal of training your eye to see everything in the frame and to understand the interaction of various cinematic elements, you may want to create a shot-by-shot analysis of a short scene.

Say, for instance, that you want to write a shot-by-shot analysis of the first five shots in Stanley Kubrick's *The Killing*. Because the opening titles appear over the action, the first shot for your analysis is the one that begins after the credit "Directed by Stanley Kubrick." You'll comment on this and the next four shots by considering some or all of the following elements:

1. Precise **location** of the shot; noteworthy aspects of the mise-en-scène
2. **Framing** of the shot (long, medium, close-up, etc.)
3. Brief description of the **action** in the shot
4. **Composition** of the frame
5. **Lighting**
6. **Camera** (static, moving, etc.)
7. **Sound** (paying particular attention to onscreen versus offscreen)
8. **Editing**

You should take notes on a chart similar to the one below, which will enable you to record and control a lot of information economically.

	Location	Framing	Action	Composition	Lighting	Camera	Sound	Editing
Shot 1								
Shot 2								
Shot 3								
Shot 4								
Shot 5								

Plot Segmentation The best method for understanding a film's narrative system is to create a *plot segmentation*, a scene-by-scene outline of the entire film. Each scene should be described briefly in a separate line, and the entire segmentation should not exceed more than a page or two. One of the first things a plot segmentation shows is the function and boundaries of the scene. Aristotle held that a scene consists of a unified time, space, and action. When a film significantly shifts in time, space, or action, we recognize that a new scene has begun. The plot segmentation helps reveal a film's overall structure (e.g., three or four acts, perhaps following a thematic pattern) and its smallest details (e.g., a motif of transitions between scenes).

Here's an excerpt from a plot segmentation of John Ford's *Stagecoach* (1939):

{Title, cast names, and principal production credits}

I. MORNING OF THE FIRST DAY IN TONTO IN THE 1870s
  A. The U.S. Calvary office receives telegraph warning that Apache warriors, under the command of Geronimo, are cutting telegraph wires, a sign that they're preparing to attack the white settlers.
  B. Six passengers, the driver, and the sheriff board the stagecoach, which is accompanied by a cavalry escort.

II. FIRST STAGE OF THE JOURNEY TO LORDSBURG
  A. Conversations establish the passengers' basic antipathy toward one another.
  B. A rifle shot announces the appearance of the Ringo Kid; he surrenders his rifle, and the sheriff arrests him as an escaped convict.
  C. Ringo enters the coach.
  D. The journey resumes without interruption.

The usefulness of this plot segmentation is twofold: First, it helps you to see the film's structure, reminding you of the scene sequence so that you don't need to keep viewing the film to determine the order of events. Second, laying the plot out in this way might help you see patterns in the film that could be useful to your paper.

Generating Ideas

While viewing a film, you will usually come up with some ideas worth writing about. But what if you've viewed a film again and again and you still haven't found anything that you feel is worth exploring? Or what if you've found an idea for writing, but you haven't yet discovered how you might develop that idea? In either of these situations you might want to take the time to try one of the following strategies for generating ideas.

Conversation After seeing a movie, we typically talk about it with others as soon as we leave the theater. Conversation about movies can help us discover what's interesting about a film. Note, however, that the kinds of conversations that we have with our friends—which are often freewheeling, opinionated, and more emotional than intellectual—mark just the beginning of scholarly inquiry. Still, talking with friends can be useful in exploring differences of opinions and in encouraging you to articulate and back up your point of view.

Brainstorming Another way to formulate ideas is to brainstorm. Brainstorming is useful because it is a quick and efficient way of laying out what you know about a subject. By brainstorming, you might also see what you *don't* know about a topic, which might move you to read and think further.

Suppose you decided to brainstorm for a paper on the film *Brokeback Mountain*. You might make a list like the one we offer here:

Brokeback Mountain

> Is controversial in its subject matter
> Is beautifully shot
> Has a lonely feeling
> Is in some ways pretty conventional
  • Has the sweeping panoramas of the western
  • Has minimal dialogue, typical of the western
  • Has the plot structure of a doomed love story
> Portrays the women as helpless
> Won the Academy Award for directing but not for best picture

As this list illustrates, *brainstorming* is an informal strategy for invention in which you jot down, as quickly as you can, ideas concerning your topic. The ideas don't have to be connected—though sometimes looking for connections will yield a paper topic. For instance, you might want to write a paper arguing that *Brokeback* is a more conventional film than most people think. Of you might want to write about how the spaces and silences of the film contribute to conveying the characters' essential loneliness.

Remember that you can also stop at any point in the writing process to brainstorm, especially when you feel that you're stuck or that you have to fill in some gaps in your argument. In short, when you brainstorm you freely explore your topic without the pressure of structure, grammar, or style. In the process, ideas for an essay (or a paragraph, or even a footnote) evolve.

Freewriting *Freewriting* is similar to brainstorming in that it is a quick and informal way to develop an idea. But whereas brainstorming most often involves making a list of ideas, freewriting requires that you try to elaborate on these ideas by writing about them, without paying attention to syntax or grammar. In this way, freewriting can get you "unstuck" when coming up with ideas is difficult.

Here's an example (and note that this writing, since it is meant for the writer's eyes only, is very informal—with spelling, grammar, and punctuation errors intact).

OK, so i just saw apocalypse now and, wow, i'm supposed to write a paper on it but i have no idea what i'm going to say. the film hit me in a place where language doesn't live but still i gotta come up with something. where to start? maybe i should begin at the beginning, because from the first scene coppola grabs you and pulls you in, not just into vietnam but also into the mind of the protagonist, willard. I mean from the start you know that it's all insane—willard's insane and so is vietnam and somehow the two insanities are the same, one is causing the other in a crazy vicious cycle. how does coppola do this? hmmmm. i guess that a lot of it has to do with the sound mix. first of all there's the great song by the doors—"the end"— which is apocalyptic and reminds us how crazy the sixties were. And willard is in this hotel room and this song is going on and we see willard sweating in this hot hotel room in Hanoi, losing his mind, and then we hear the ceiling fan that swoops menacingly overhead. And the fan blurs with the sounds of helicopters and the other sounds of the war. And you feel like the sounds outside and the sounds inside are all blending into each other. And then at the height of the insanity willard tears up the hotel room, breaks a mirror, bleeds on the sheets, and lets out a howl, which you don't hear. that's cool. you watch willard fall apart but you don't hear him screaming. you hear all the other stuff but you don't hear the scream. i wonder why coppola decided to do it this way? maybe i could think more about the sound editing in that first scene, maybe do a paper on that and how coppola manages to reflect with sound the inner and outer insanities? hmmmm. i guess this was a pretty successful freewrite. all i had to do was push buttons and some ideas popped out. pushing buttons is a lot more fun than just sitting and staring at a blank screen.

Discovery Draft A discovery draft is a third strategy for coming up with or developing your ideas. A *discovery draft* is similar to freewriting in that you can write freely, ignoring the structure and the development of your ideas for the time being. You can also forget about matters of syntax and style.

However, writing a discovery draft is different from freewriting in that a discovery draft makes a conscious attempt to focus on and develop an idea or cluster of ideas. In other words, a discovery draft is like freewriting with an agenda. Because you have an agenda, discovery drafts tend to be more structured than freewritings. They also tend to be written more or less coherently, in complete sentences.

Think of writing a discovery draft as writing a letter to an imaginary friend about your paper. Suppose that you've just seen *Memento*. You might first summarize, for your friend's benefit, the film and the issues it presents. You might then raise questions about the film. You might challenge the filmmaker on certain points. You might note continuity problems or contradictions. You might point out a certain part of the film that you found compelling. You might address and then work out any confusion that you have about the topic. In writing the discovery draft you might have an aha! moment, in which you see something you hadn't seen before, and break off midsentence to explore it.

In a sense, the aha! moment is the point of the discovery draft. When writing the discovery draft, your thoughts are focused on your topic. You're giving language to your questions and observations. In this process, the mind almost always stumbles across something new—makes a *discovery*. And with this discovery, a paper is often launched.

Five *W*s and an *H* Journalism has provided us with perhaps the simplest and most familiar way of coming up with a topic: simply ask questions like *who, what, when, where, why,* and *how*. Answering these questions initially doesn't seem very hard—at least, until one gets to the *why* and *how*. Then it gets tricky.

Let's use this method to try to generate ideas, once again, for a paper on Francis Ford Coppola's *Apocalypse Now*. Maybe when you were watching *Apocalypse Now* you got interested in Coppola's use of voice-over, so you have a topic you want to explore. Now begin your interrogation:

> **Where** in the film does Coppola use voice-over? (Mark the scenes.)
> **What** was happening in those moments? (Summarize the action.)
> **How** is the voice-over used? (Analyze. Is Coppola using the voice-over to restore order when the narrative slips into chaos?)
> **When** does the voice-over work best? (Evaluate its effectiveness. Is order really restored?)
> **Why** does the film end without a final voice-over comment? Why does it end in silence?

These are tough questions. But it's precisely when you have difficulty answering a *why* question that a real paper is beginning. When the answer comes too easily, you're on familiar ground, so you're probably not saying anything interesting. Cultivate a taste for confusion. Then cultivate a strategy for clearing up confusion. Only when you ask a question that initially confuses you can real thinking and real writing begin.

Tagmemics *Tagmemics* is a system that allows you to look at a single object from three different perspectives. One of these perspectives (or even all three) can help you determine a subject for writing. Tagmemics involves seeing your topic

> As a **particle** (as a thing in itself)
> As a **wave** (as a thing changing over time)
> As **part of a field** (as a thing in its context)

Suppose you want to write a paper on Cooper and Schoedsack's *King Kong* (1933). If you use tagmemics as a system of invention, you will begin by looking at *King Kong* as a thing in itself. In other words, what elements of this 1933 film are worth noting?

Next you might consider how the film has changed over time. How was the film received in its day? How does this reception compare to current assessments of the film? Consider the Peter Jackson remake (2005). What elements of the film have changed in the remake? How has the approach to the King Kong story changed over time?

Finally, consider *King Kong* (1933) as a thing in context. Relate it to its culture, to its moment in time. What was happening in the world in 1933? Even unlikely events and figures may provide an interesting context. For instance, in 1933 the United States was in the middle of the Great Depression, and Hitler was named chancellor of Germany. Might these events be reflected in the film in some way? How? And why?

Aristotle's *Topoi* As one of the fathers of rhetoric, Aristotle worked to formalize a system for coming up with, organizing, and expressing ideas. We're concerned here with what Aristotle called the *topoi*—a system of specific strategies for invention. Think of the *topoi* as a series of questions that you might ask of a film—questions that might lead you to interesting paper topics. The *topoi* are especially helpful when you're asked to explore a topic that seems very broad. Consider, for instance, how using the *topoi* can help you write a paper on the importance of *Star Wars* to the sci-fi genre.

Use Definition

You can use definition in two ways to come up with or develop a topic. First, you might look at *genus*, which Aristotle explains as defining a general idea within specific limits. For example, you could define the sci-fi genre with the intent of showing how *Star Wars* epitomizes the elements of that genre.

The second way to use definition is to think in terms of *division*. In other words, try to think of your subject in terms of its parts. For example, consider the elements of *Star Wars* that are most significant in earning it the reputation of the most important science fiction film in movie history.

Use Comparison

You can generate ideas by making comparisons in two ways. The first is to look for *similarities* and/or *differences*. For example, you might determine how *Star Wars* stands apart from other important sci-fi films.

The second method is to compare *degree*. In other words, you might consider how something is better or worse than something else. For example, is *Star Wars* more important to the genre than *The Matrix*? Is it is less important to the genre than *2001: A Space Odyssey*?

Explore Relationships

Aristotle determined four ways of exploring relationships as a way of coming up with ideas for writing. The first is to consider either the *cause* of your subject or its *effects*. For example, you might research the effects that *Star Wars* had on subsequent sci-fi films.

Second, you might consider a subject's *antecedent* and *consequences*. In other words, you might ask this question of your subject: If this, then what? For example, if *Star Wars* hadn't been made, would science fiction movies still be stuck in the B movie genre?

Third, you might examine *contraries*, or make an argument by proving its opposite. An example is to say that war is bad in order to convey the idea that peace is good. Along these lines, you might argue that *Star Wars* was the most significant sci-fi film of all time by showing how others miss the mark.

Finally, you might look for *contradictions*, *incompatible statements*, or *controversy*. For example, some critics feel that *Star Wars* is the greatest sci-fi film of all time; others feel that it's overrated. You can explore the controversy and stake a claim of your own.

Examine Circumstances

In seeking an idea for a paper, you can examine circumstances in two ways. The first is to consider the possible and the impossible. Sometimes you can construct an interesting argument by considering what's possible and what's not. For example, it's impossible to find a sci-fi series that is more influential to the genre than the *Star Wars* series.

The second strategy is to consider the past or to look to the future. For example, in what ways does *Star Wars* influence the sci-fi films being produced today? What trends do we see that might allow us to predict the direction of future sci-fi films?

Rely on Testimony
The opinions of others can be a source for your paper. Look to authorities, testimonials, statistics, maxims, laws, and precedents. For example, read what Joseph Campbell says on the mythic/heroic structure of *Star Wars*. Find other authorities and listen to what they have to say. For instance, what does the box-office history of *Star Wars* tell us about its success?

Focusing Your Ideas

You've done some preliminary brainstorming. Perhaps you've even completed a discovery draft. The problem sitting before you now is that you have too many ideas and you don't know what to do with them. Or the ideas you've come up with don't seem to be adequately academic. What do you try next?

Nutshelling *Nutshelling* is the simple process of trying to explain the main point of your observations in a few sentences—in a nutshell. When you put your thoughts in a nutshell, you come to see just how those thoughts fit together. You see how each thought is relevant to the others, and what the overall "point" is. In short, nutshelling helps you transform your observations or information into something meaningful, focused, and coherent.

Imagine, for example, that you're asked in an assignment to consider whether or not, from your point of view, Philip Seymour Hoffman deserved to win the Best Actor Oscar for his portrayal of Truman Capote in the film *Capote*. You actually have a lot to say about this. First, though Hoffman's performance was superb (in fact, you loved it), you think that Heath Ledger's portrayal of a gay cowboy in *Brokeback Mountain* was more Oscar-worthy. Why? Well, when you were watching *Brokeback*, you forgot you were watching Heath Ledger play a gay cowboy; when you were watching *Capote*, you were always aware that you were watching Hoffman taking on Capote's skin. In your opinion, making the audience forget that they're watching a celebrity is harder than imitating (however brilliantly) another celebrity. But you're pretty sure the academy doesn't agree with you. After all, they recently gave the Oscar to Nicole Kidman for playing Virginia Woolf, and to Jamie Foxx for playing Ray Charles.

In a nutshell, what is your take on the matter? After considering all of your feelings on the subject, you decide that, although Philip Seymour Hoffman's performance was Oscar-worthy, his win over Heath Ledger reveals how celebrity-obsessed the voting members of the academy are. Stated more fully,

> When actors in biopics meet the challenges of recreating a character, they dazzle us: it seems as if they've managed to resurrect their subjects before our very eyes. And yet this resurrection shouldn't be the determining criterion for awarding the Oscar, as it has been in the last few years. Philip Seymour Hoffman's win over Heath Ledger's in the 2006 Oscar race illustrates the tendency of Oscar voters to reward celebrities playing other celebrities, indicating the Academy's own obsession with celebrity culture.

In the process of nutshelling you've done more than come up with a promising idea for a paper, you've also come up with a promising plan for your entire introduction. Nutshelling has proven to be a successful prewriting strategy in this case.

Broadening Your Topic What happens when you've put your thoughts in a nutshell and they seem too "small"? You may have come up with a topic that's too narrow, too particular to support a sustained conversation.

Say, for example, that you've been asked to watch a film and to observe the makeup and costuming. You've noticed that the filmmaker seems to focus on women and lipstick. The film has a key scene of women discussing their sex lives as they try on lipstick at a cosmetics counter. Throughout the film, the director makes sure that we notice lipstick by offering lingering close-ups of women putting on lipstick, of lipstick stains on glasses, and so on.

You've made notes about these lipstick scenes, and you think that you can write an essay that chronicles the use of lipstick as a metaphor in this film. But it's not enough simply to chronicle the appearance of lipstick in the film. Instead, you have to talk about *how* the director uses these images and then make a declaration about what this recurring image *means*.

After writing your discovery draft, you come up with the idea that the filmmaker uses lipstick to call attention to the fact that the characters are trying to mask their feelings. Though this observation is a promising one, it still isn't "big" enough. Why not? Because it remains an observation, not an argument; it lists *how* A, B, and C mask their feelings without addressing the matter of *why* this masking is important to consider. How do you broaden your topic so that you feel you have something important to say?

First, try to make connections. Do the characters rely on other ways of masking themselves? Is masking one of the film's central themes? In what other ways does the director explore the idea of masking?

Second, turn your idea inside out. Consider the other side of the matter. For example, lipstick might be part of a character's mask, but it also calls attention to that character. Lipstick doesn't give her a mask to hide behind; instead it screams, "Hey! Look at me!" This is interesting. Perhaps the character exaggerates certain qualities in order to hide others. Is this sleight of hand (reveal/conceal) at work elsewhere in the film?

Third, consider the context. There are, of course, at least two contexts to consider: the context *within* the film, and the context *without*. With*in* the film, you might seek a context for lipstick. What's happening, exactly, when the characters put lipstick on? Is this act presented by the filmmaker as being positive or negative? What values does the film assert, and how does the use of lipstick reflect or challenge these values? What is the film's theme, and how does lipstick reflect or challenge that?

With*out* the film are other contexts. Consider, for instance, the filmmaker's other works. Is masking an important issue there? Consider some of the cultural forces at work. What larger social issue might the filmmaker be highlighting? Finally, masking is an ancient practice. What can you find out about the history of masking that is relevant to the matter at hand?

All of these questions might help you broaden your topic so that your discussion is substantial and interesting.

Narrowing/Focusing Your Topic What if your topic seems too big to handle? What do you do then?

Let's consider the hypothetical film that we were just discussing. Perhaps after doing the various prewriting exercises, you've concluded that all the characters in this film seem to wear masks. Although this observation is potentially fruitful, you should resist the temptation to be satisfied with it. After all, a paper showing that Mary wears a mask and Johnny wears a mask and Caroline wears a mask will probably bore the reader. It will seem like a string of obvious and general observations. How do you focus your topic?

First, test your claim. A statement as broad as this one is probably not always true. Do all the characters wear masks, or just some of them? You might discover that only the female characters wear masks. Or you might discover that, while these women wear makeup (a kind of physical mask), it's the men in the film whose feelings are most concealed. These more focused observations lead to a more interesting, more manageable topic.

Then look for examples. Remember that broad is also *vague*. Focusing on specific examples can make a topic clearer. For example, you might want to consider when, specifically, the characters try to mask themselves. Do they mask themselves in every moment of the film, or only at those moments that are crucial to their destinies? Are they cowards, or is the filmmaker trying to say that it's right for people to try to protect themselves from the cruelty of fate?

Look for more examples. How do people mask themselves? Reconsider the lipstick idea. Perhaps the use of lipstick in the film signifies the impulse to mask.

Finally, consider the context. Just as a consideration of context can help you broaden an idea, it can also help you focus it. "Everybody masks" can therefore become, "Historically, people have used masks in these particular ways. Filmmaker X uses masks in similar ways to argue Y." Then show (1) how the characters use masks in traditional ways, and (2) what the filmmaker is trying to illustrate through these allusions to the historical uses of the mask.

Thinking Beyond the Frame So far, we've been advising you to consider the formal aspects of a film's composition. As we pointed out earlier, however, you can write about film in several ways. Sometimes you will want to "think beyond the frame" and consider questions about how the film was made, its historical context, and so on. For example, ask yourself the following questions:

> **Who made the film?** Find out who directed the film and what other films this director has made. If you've seen some of these other films, you'll have a better understanding of the themes and genres that interest the director.

> **What is the production history of the film?** See if you can find out anything about the conditions under which the film was made. *Apocalypse Now*, for example, has an interesting production history, in terms of its financing, casting, writing, and so on. Knowing something about the film's production can help you understand some of the aesthetic and cinematic choices that the director has made.

> **What do the critics and scholars say?** Reading what others have said about the film before you see it may help you focus your observations. If a film is particularly well known for the editing of a certain scene (the shower scene in Hitchcock's *Psycho*, for example), you'll want to pay close attention to the editing when you view the film.

> **What can you learn from the film's genre?** Before you see the film, think a bit about the norms and limitations of its genre. When you view the film, you can then consider how these limitations are obeyed

or stretched. For example, Clint Eastwood's *Unforgiven* is a western that challenges its genre's typical notions of good guy versus bad guy. Knowing how this dynamic plays itself out in other westerns helps you understand and appreciate Eastwood's accomplishment.

> **Does the film reflect an interesting cultural phenomenon?** Sometimes a professor will ask you to watch certain films because he wants you to examine a cultural phenomenon—for example, the phenomenon of stardom. Accordingly, you might watch Roland Joffé's *The Scarlet Letter* with the idea of viewing it as a "star vehicle," contributing to Demi Moore's star persona. Note that this sort of paper may also be a discussion of formal analysis; for example, you might discuss how Demi Moore was lit in certain scenes to emphasize her position as Hollywood star.

Researching Film

Doing research in a film class is in many ways similar to doing research for other classes. One important difference is that, when you write about movies, the motion picture is typically the primary source, with film criticism (books, journal articles, and so on) serving as secondary sources.

Understanding Primary and Secondary Sources *Primary sources* are defined as any text, object, photograph, film, or other media that is the object of scholarly investigation. A *secondary source*, on the other hand, is a work that analyzes, comments on, or otherwise sheds light on the primary text, historical event, object, or phenomenon in question. A source can be primary or secondary, depending on the purpose of your research. For instance, you might write a film paper in which the primary text is something other than a movie (e.g., a filmmaker's journal, shooting script, or shot list). Or you might write a paper in which a secondary source consists of film footage (e.g., a DVD extra).

Using Sources

Summarize Your Sources

Before attempting to use any source in your paper, make sure you understand it. The best way to do this is to summarize the source. In summarizing, you accomplish a few things. First, summarizing a source requires you to put the argument in your own language. Some of your secondary sources might use language that puzzles you. When you summarize, you are, in a sense, translating an argument into language that you understand and can work with. Summarizing also helps you see whether there's any aspect of the argument that you *don't* understand. If you find yourself stumbling as you attempt to summarize, go back to the original source for clarity.

Summarizing also allows you to restate an argument in terms that are relevant to your paper. Most films and film criticism that you encounter are very complex and offer several ideas for consideration. Some of these ideas will be relevant to your topic; others will not. When you summarize, you can restate the part of the argument that seems most relevant to the paper you want to write.

Summarizing can also help you organize your source material. If you've used ten sources in a research project, you've probably taken a lot of notes and have gathered several quotations for your paper. This can amount to pages and pages of text. Summaries can help you organize these notes by telling you almost at a glance which idea comes from which source. You can also include in your summaries the two or three best quotations from each source.

Finally, summarizing is helpful to the entire research process. It's not something that you should do once at the beginning of the research process and then forget about. Every time your understanding of the topic shifts or evolves, take the time to write a brief summary. You'll find that putting your thoughts into writing helps you solidify one stage of understanding before progressing to the next.

Categorize Your Sources

Once you've summarized your sources, try to place them into various categories. Remember, writing an academic essay is like taking part in a large, ongoing conversation. Although everyone has a particular point of view, it's safe to say that no one is entering the conversation as a lone wolf. Everyone is speaking from a certain critical perspective. These perspectives might be classified into different groups.

Categorizing your sources might be as simple as looking for similarities among them. Which of these sources seem to share a point of view? Which seem to arrive at similar conclusions? You will also discover differences among your sources. Try to define these differences and see if they seem to fall into different categories. For example, side A seems to believe X, while side B seems to believe Y. Or side A attempts to understand the problem from a feminist perspective, while side B is interested in rooting the problem in socioeconomic terms, and side C is arguing that the problem doesn't even exist.

Once you've categorized your sources, try to understand what these differences and similarities mean to your argument. Are these categories relevant to the matter you intend to discuss? Where does your own argument fit in? Does the reader need to know about these categories in order for your argument to make sense? Try to articulate these matters clearly. Write a summary of what you think at this point.

Interrogate Your Sources

In most of the papers that you'll write in college, you'll have to do more than review what other people have said about a topic. You will be asked to present your own point of view, and to do this, you'll need to interrogate your sources.

Interrogating your sources does not mean that you have to be contentious. You don't have to search like a bloodhound for the weak spot in an argument. You're not required to "take on" your source. Instead, you'll want to ask questions of your sources. Initiate a conversation. Challenge, interrogate, rebut, confirm. Here are some good questions to ask:

> - Is the writer offering evidence for her claims? Is this evidence sufficient? Why or why not?
> - Is there something that the writer is overlooking? Omitting? If so, is the omission a matter of carelessness, or does it seem purposeful? Why?
> - Does the writer's argument seem reasonable? If not, can you locate places where the reason seems to break down? Can you locate and identify any logical fallacies?
> - Is the writer's language appropriate? Does she sometimes rely on a pretty phrase or a passionate claim to cover up a lack of evidence?
> - What can you determine about the writer's perspective? Does she seem to have any important biases? Does she seem to belong to a particular critical school? Does the writer's perspective help or hinder the argument she's trying to make? Why?
> - Where do you stand in relation to the writer? Do you give her a round of applause? Do you feel like booing her off the stage? Are you sitting with your arms crossed, feeling skeptical? Keep notes of your personal responses to the writer, and try to translate those responses into comments or questions.

Make Your Sources Work for You

Students often make a grave mistake when they write their first academic papers: overwhelmed by what their sources have to say, they permit their papers to crumble under the weight of scholarly opinion. They end up not writing an informed argument of their own, but rehashing what has already been said on a topic. The paper might be informative. It might also be competently written. But it does not fulfill the requirements of a good academic paper.

You've heard this before, but it bears repeating: A good academic paper must be analytical. It must be critical. It must be a well-crafted, persuasive, *informed argument.*

Consider the phrase *informed argument.* The word with the power in this phrase is the noun, *argument.* The word *informed* is merely a descriptor. It serves the noun, qualifying it, shading it. The information that you gather should serve your argument in much the same way. Make your sources work for *you.*

You can take some steps to ensure that your sources do indeed work for you without overwhelming your argument. First, don't go to the library or go online before you've thought about your topic on your own. Certainly your research will have an impact on what you think. Sometimes you might even find that you reverse your opinion. But if you go to the library before you've given your topic some thought, you risk jumping on the bandwagon of the first persuasive argument you encounter.

Second, limit your sources to those that are relevant to your topic. It's easy to be swept up in the broader scholarly conversation about your subject and to go off on tangents that don't, in the end, serve your argument.

Finally, keep track of your evolving understanding of the topic by periodically stopping to summarize. As we said earlier, summarizing your sources makes them more manageable. If you manage your sources as you go along, you reduce the risk that they'll overwhelm you later.

Keeping Track of Sources During the research process it's very important to keep track of your sources. Nothing is more frustrating than having a great quotation and not knowing where it came from. Develop a good, consistent system for keeping notes.

Every academic discipline requires that you submit with your paper a bibliography or list of works cited. A bibliography should include every work you looked at in your research, even if you didn't quote that source directly. A list of works cited, on the other hand, is just that: a list of works that you quoted, paraphrased, or alluded to when writing your paper. Both bibliographies and lists of works cited require you to provide information that will make it easier for your reader to find sources for herself. Consult the *MLA* (Modern Language Association) *Handbook* for information about how to construct a proper bibliography and/or list of works cited.

Citing Sources When you write an academic paper, you must cite all the sources that you've used. If you fail to cite these sources, you will be charged with plagiarism. *Plagiarism* (passing off as your own the words and ideas of others—whether an entire article or just one sentence) is an academic offense for which there are serious consequences.

There are several good reasons not to plagiarize. First, it's very easy to get caught. Your instructors—who have spent years teaching students to write and so have read countless student essays—are keenly aware of the difference between professional and student writing. They notice when wonderful academic writing appears out of the blue, with seemingly no development or context. In addition, Internet technologies (the same ones that make plagiarism so easy) also empower teachers, who can utilize sophisticated search programs to scan literally millions of documents for suspect phrases and sentences.

Second, plagiarism cheats everyone: both the reader and the writer. At a fundamental level, citing a source is an academic courtesy. Because scholarship is an ongoing conversation, you should always presume that other students or scholars could want to use your work to develop their own. If you've taken an idea from another scholar but haven't cited it (or have cited it improperly), your reader will have no easy way of finding the source of the ideas that have found their way into your work.

Perhaps the most serious problem raised when you plagiarize or fail to cite your sources is that you're cheating yourself. When you rely on the ideas of others to meet a course requirement, you're denying yourself the opportunity to have the best experience that college can offer: the opportunity to think for yourself. Writing papers can be difficult, and when deadlines loom it can be tempting to look for a shortcut and to lift ideas from scholars who clearly know more about your topic than you do. But it's *your* opinion that your instructor wants to hear. Take each writing assignment as an opportunity to explore and express your ideas. You're paying a lot for this education; you might as well get your money's worth.

Developing Your Thesis

Writing a Thesis Sentence No sentence in your paper will vex you as much as the thesis sentence, and with good reason: the thesis sentence is typically the *one* sentence in the paper that asserts, controls, and structures the entire argument. Without a strong, persuasive, thoughtful thesis, a paper might seem unfocused, weak, and not worth the reader's time.

What makes a good thesis sentence? A good thesis sentence generally has the following characteristics:

> **A good thesis sentence makes a claim.** This doesn't mean that you have to reduce an idea to an either/or proposition and then take a stand. Rather, you need to develop an interesting perspective that you can support and defend. This perspective must be more than

an observation. "America is violent" is an observation. "Americans are violent because they are fearful" (the position that Michael Moore takes in *Bowling for Columbine*) is an argument. Why? Because it posits a perspective. It makes a claim. Put another way, a good thesis sentence inspires (rather than quieting) other points of view. One might argue that America is violent because of its violent entertainment industry. Or because of the proliferation of guns. Or because of the disintegration of the family. In short, if your thesis is positing something that no one can (or would wish to) argue with, then it's not a very good thesis.

> **A good thesis sentence controls the entire argument.** The thesis sentence determines what you're required to say in a paper. It also determines what you cannot say. Every paragraph in your paper exists to support your thesis. Accordingly, if one paragraph you've written seems irrelevant to your thesis, you have two choices: get rid of it or rewrite the thesis sentence. Understand that you don't have a third option: you can't simply include the idea without preparing the reader for it in your thesis. The thesis is like a contract between you and your reader. If you introduce ideas that the reader isn't prepared for, you've violated that contract.

> **A good thesis sentence provides a structure for the argument.** The thesis sentence signals to the reader not only what your argument is, but how it will be presented. In other words, your thesis sentence should either directly or indirectly suggest the structure of your argument to the reader. Say, for example, that you're going to argue that "Michael Moore plays on American fearfulness by using three techniques: A, B, and C." In this case, the reader understands that you're going to cover three important points, and that these points will appear in a certain order. If you suggest a particular ordering principle and then abandon it, the reader will feel betrayed, irritated, and confused.

Alternatives to the Thesis Sentence Sometimes the purpose of a piece of writing is not to make a claim but to raise questions. Other times a writer wants to leave a matter unresolved, inspiring readers to create their own positions. In these cases, the thesis sentence might take other forms: the *thesis question* or the *implied thesis*.

The Thesis Question
As we've said, not every piece of writing sets out to make a claim. If your purpose as a writer is to explore, for instance, the reasons for the success of *The Passion* (a topic for which you're not prepared to make a claim), your

thesis might read, "What cultural forces conspired to make this movie a blockbuster hit?"

Note that this question, while provocative, does not offer a sense of the argument's structure. It permits the writer to pursue all ideas, without committing to any. Although this freedom might seem appealing, in fact you will find that the lack of a declarative thesis statement requires *more* work: you need to tighten your internal structure and your transitions from paragraph to paragraph so that the essay is clear and the reader can easily follow your line of inquiry.

The Implied Thesis

One of the most fascinating things about a thesis sentence is that it is the most important sentence in a paper—even when it's not there.

Some of the best writers never explicitly declare a thesis. In some essays, you'll find it difficult to point to a single sentence that declares the argument. Still, the essay is coherent and makes a point. In these cases the writers have used an implied thesis.

Writers use an implied thesis when they want readers to come to their own conclusions about the matter at hand. However, just because the writer doesn't declare the thesis doesn't mean that she was working without one. Good writers will clearly state a thesis—either in their own minds or in their notes for the paper. They may elect not to put the thesis in the paper, but every paragraph, every sentence, that they write is controlled by the thesis all the same.

If you decide to write a paper with an implied thesis, be sure that you have a strong grasp of your argument and its structure. Also be sure that you supply adequate transitions so that the reader can follow your argument with ease.

The Thesis Sentence Checklist In the end, you may have spent a good deal of time writing your thesis and still not know if it's a good one. Here are some questions to ask yourself:

> Does the thesis sentence attempt to answer (or at least to explore) a challenging intellectual question?
> Will the point I'm making generate discussion and argument, or will it leave people asking, "So what?"
> Is the thesis too vague? Too general? Should I focus on a more specific aspect of the topic?
> Does the thesis deal directly with the topic at hand, or is it a declaration of my personal feelings?

> Does the thesis indicate the direction of my argument? Does it suggest a structure for my paper?
> Does the introductory paragraph define terms important to my thesis? If I'm writing a research paper, does the introduction "place" my thesis within the larger, ongoing scholarly discussion about the topic?

Considering Structure and Organization

Organizing Your Thoughts Once you've figured out what you want to say, you're left with the problem of how to say it. How should you begin the paper? Should you address the opinions of other thinkers? And what should you do with that stubborn contradiction you've uncovered in your own thinking?

Writing papers in college requires that you come up with sophisticated, complex, and even creative ways of structuring your ideas. Accordingly, we can't offer simple formulas that will work for every paper, every time. We can, however, give you some things to think about that will help you as you consider how to structure your paper.

Let Your Thesis Direct You

Begin by listening to your thesis. If it's well written, it will tell you which way to go with your paper. Suppose, for example, that, in responding to the films of the early Soviet filmmakers, you have written a thesis that says this:

> The purpose of the early Soviet films was not only to support the ideology of the revolution, but to create *Homo sovieticus*, a new kind of human being.

This thesis provides the writer with several clues about how best to structure the paper, and prepares the readers for what they will encounter in the paper. First, the thesis promises readers that the paper will argue that Soviet filmmakers were interested in more than ideology. The paper will therefore begin by acknowledging that, although the promotion of Soviet values was important to these filmmakers, it was not their only goal. The rest of the paper will concern the (more important) creation of *Homo sovieticus*—or Soviet human being.

We say that this idea of *Homo sovieticus* is more important than ideology not because the Soviet filmmakers thought so, but because the writer seems to say so in her thesis. Read the thesis sentence again. Note that the emphasis falls on the last phrase: "a new kind of human being." The emphasis in this sentence dictates the emphasis of the entire paper. As readers, we expect that the other issues taken up in this paper will be discussed in terms of creating *Homo sovieticus*. In other words, we will be given not simply a description of how Soviet filmmakers propagate Soviet ideology, but a description of how this ideology was used to create the new Soviet person.

Sketching Your Argument Although your thesis will identify your paper's general direction, it will not necessarily provide you with a plan for how to organize all of your points, large and small. Here it might be helpful to diagram or sketch your argument.

In sketching your argument, the goal is to fill the page with your ideas. Begin by writing your thesis. Put it where your instincts tell you to: at the top of the page, in the center, at the bottom. Around the thesis, cluster the points you want to make. Under each of these points, note the observations you've made and the evidence you'll use. Don't get nervous when your sketch starts to look messy. Use arrows. Draw circles. Take up colored pens. Any of these methods can help you find connections between your ideas that otherwise might go unnoticed. Working from your sketch, try to see the line of reasoning that is evolving.

Sketching is an important step in the writing process because it allows you to explore visually the connections between your ideas. If you outline a paper too early in the process, you risk missing these connections. You line up your points—A, B, C—without fully understanding why. Sketching your argument helps you see, for example, that points A and C really overlap and need to be thought through more carefully.

Outlining Your Argument When you've finished the sketch, you're ready to make an outline. The task of the outline is to identify the paper's "best structure." By *best structure* we mean the structure that best supports the argument you intend to make.

When you're outlining a paper, you'll have many options for organization. Understand, however, that each choice you make eliminates dozens of other options. Your goal is to come up with an outline in which all your choices support your thesis.

Treat the outline as if it were a puzzle that you were trying to put together. In a puzzle, each piece has only one appropriate place. The same should be true of your paper. If it's easy to shift around your ideas—if paragraph five and paragraph nine could be switched around and no one would be the wiser—then you haven't yet found the best structure for your paper. Keep working until your outline fits your ideas like a glove.

When you think you have an outline that works, challenge it. The first outline rarely holds up to a good interrogation. When you start asking questions of your outline, you will begin to see where the plan holds and where it falls apart. Here are some questions you might ask:

> Does my thesis control the direction of the outline?
> Are all of my main points relevant to the thesis?
> Can any of these points be moved around without changing something important about the thesis?
> Does the outline seem logical?
> Does the argument progress, or does it stall?
> If the argument seems to take a turn midstream, does the thesis anticipate that turn?
> Do I have sufficient support for each of my points?
> Have I made room in the outline for other points of view about the topic?
> Does this outline reflect a thorough, thoughtful argument? Have I covered the ground?

Constructing Paragraphs Imagine that you've written the thesis. You've interrogated the outline. You know which modes of arrangement you intend to use. You've settled on a plan that you think will work. Now you have to go about the serious business of constructing paragraphs.

You were probably told in high school that paragraphs are the workhorses of a paper. Indeed they are. If a single paragraph is incoherent or weak, the entire argument might fail. It's important that you consider carefully the "job" of each paragraph. Know what you want that paragraph to do. Don't allow it to go off loafing.

What Is a Paragraph?
A *paragraph* is generally understood as a single "unit" of a paper. What your readers expect when they enter a new paragraph is that you're going to declare a point and then offer support for that point. If you violate this expectation—if your paragraphs wander aimlessly among a half dozen points, or if they declare points without offering any evidence to support them—readers will become confused or irritated by your argument. They won't want to read any further.

What Should a Paragraph Do?
At the risk of sounding silly, we suggest that you consider this: What you look for in a boyfriend or girlfriend, a reader looks for in a paragraph. You want a partner who is supportive, strong, and considerate to others. Similarly, a good paragraph is

> **Supportive.** Even in the most trying of times a good paragraph finds a way to support the thesis. It declares its relationship to the thesis

clearly, so that the whole world knows what the paragraph intends to do. In other words, *a supportive paragraph's main idea clearly develops the argument of the thesis.*

> **Strong.** A good paragraph isn't bloated with irrelevant evidence or redundant sentences. Nor is it a scrawny thing, begging to be fed. It's strong and buffed. You know that it's been worked on. In other words, *a strong paragraph develops its main idea, using sufficient evidence.*

> **Considerate.** Good paragraphs consider their relationship to other paragraphs. A good paragraph never interrupts its fellow paragraphs to babble on about its own, irrelevant problems. A good paragraph waits its turn. It shows up when and where it's supposed to. It doesn't make a mess for other paragraphs to clean up. In other words, *a considerate paragraph is a coherent paragraph. It makes sense within the text as a whole.*

Writing the Topic Sentence Just as every paper requires a thesis sentence to assert and control its argument, so also every paragraph requires a topic sentence to assert and control its main idea. Without a topic sentence, your paragraphs will seem jumbled, aimless. Your reader will become confused.

Because the topic sentence plays an important role in your paragraph, it must be crafted with care. When you've written a topic sentence, ask yourself the following questions:

> **Does the topic sentence declare a single point of the argument?** Because the reader expects that a paragraph will explore only one idea in your paper, it's important that your topic sentence not be too ambitious. If it points to two or three ideas, perhaps you need to consider developing more paragraphs.

> **Does the topic sentence further the argument?** Give your topic sentences the same "so what?" test that you gave your thesis sentence. If your topic sentence isn't interesting, your paragraph probably won't further the argument. Your paper could stall.

> **Is the topic sentence relevant to the thesis?** It might seem so to you, but the relevance may not be so clear to your reader. If you find that your topic sentence is taking you into new ground, stop writing and consider your options. Either you'll have to rewrite your thesis to accommodate this new direction, or you'll have to exclude this paragraph from your final paper.

> **Is there a clear relationship between this topic sentence and the paragraph that came before?** Make sure that you haven't left out any steps in the process of composing your argument. If you take a sudden turn in your reasoning, signify that turn to the reader by

using the proper transitional phrase—*on the other hand, however,* or the like.

> **Does the topic sentence control the paragraph?** If your paragraph seems to unravel, take a second look. Perhaps the topic sentence isn't adequately controlling the paragraph and needs to be rewritten. Or maybe the paragraph is moving on to a new idea that needs to be sorted out.

> **Where have I placed my topic sentence?** Usually a topic sentence comes at the beginning of a paragraph. A reader expects to see it there, so if you're going to place it elsewhere, you'll need to have a good reason and a bit of skill. You might justify putting the topic sentence in the middle of the paragraph—for example, if you have information that needs to precede it. You might also justify putting the topic sentence at the end of the paragraph, if you want the reader to consider your line of reasoning before you declare your main point.

Developing Your Argument: Evidence Students often ask how long a paragraph ought to be. To this we respond, "As long as it takes."

It's possible to make a point quickly. Sometimes it's desirable to keep it short. Notice the preceding paragraph, for example. We might have hemmed and hawed, talked about short paragraphs and long paragraphs. We might have said that the average paragraph is one-half to two-thirds of a page in length. We might have spent time explaining why the too-short paragraph is too short, and the too-long paragraph too long. Instead, we cut to the chase. After huffing and puffing through this paragraph (which is getting longer and longer all the time), we'll give you the same advice: a good paragraph is as long as it needs to be in order to illustrate, explore, and/or prove its main idea.

However, length isn't all that matters in paragraph development. What's important is that a paragraph develop its idea fully, and in a manner that readers can follow with ease.

Let's consider these two issues carefully. First, how do we know when an idea is fully developed? If your topic sentence is well written, it should tell you what the paragraph needs to do. If the topic sentence declares, for example, that there are two conflicting impulses at work in a particular fictional character, then the reader will expect the two impulses to be defined and illustrated. It might take two paragraphs to do this; it might take one. The decision will depend on how important this matter is to the discussion. If the point is important, you'll take your time, and (more likely than not) you'll use at least two paragraphs. In this case, a topic sentence might be understood as controlling not only a paragraph, but an entire section of text.

When you've written a paragraph, ask yourself the following questions:

> Do I have enough evidence to support this paragraph's idea?
> Do I have too much evidence? In other words, will the reader be lost in a morass of details, unable to see the argument as a whole?
> Does this evidence clearly support the assertion that I'm making in this paragraph, or am I stretching it?
> If I'm stretching it, what can I do to persuade the reader that this stretch is worth making?
> Am I repeating myself in this paragraph?
> Have I defined all of the paragraph's important terms?
> Can I say, in a nutshell, what the purpose of this paragraph is?
> Has the paragraph fulfilled that purpose?

Developing Your Argument: Arrangement Equally important to the idea of a paragraph's development is the matter of the paragraph's arrangement. Paragraphs are arranged differently for different purposes. For example, if you're writing a paper about a film's history and wish to summarize a sequence of events, of course you'll arrange the information chronologically. If you're writing a paper in which you want to describe the composition of a frame or scene, perhaps you'll choose to arrange the information spatially. If you're writing a paper about the elements of a film that make it stand out from other films in its genre, you might want to arrange your ideas by working from the specific to the general. And so on.

Coherence So, you have your thesis, your topic sentences, and truckloads of evidence to support the whole lot. You've spent three days writing your paragraphs, making sure that each paragraph argues one point and that this point is well supported with textual evidence. But when you read the essay back to yourself, you feel a profound sense of disappointment. Though you've followed your outline, the essay just doesn't seem to hold together. It could be that you have a problem with coherence.

A lack of coherence is easy to diagnose but not so easy to cure. An incoherent essay doesn't seem to flow. Its arguments are hard to understand. The reader has to double back again and again in order to follow the gist of the argument. Something has gone wrong. What?

Look for the following issues in your paper:

> **Make sure the grammatical subjects of your sentences reflect the real subject of your paragraph.** Underline the subjects of all the sentences in the paragraph. Do these subjects match the paragraph's

subject in most cases? Or have you put the paragraph's subject into another, less important part of the sentence? Remember that the reader understands an idea's importance according to where you place it. If your main idea is hidden as an object of a preposition in a subordinate clause, do you really think your reader is going to follow what you're trying to say?

> **Make sure the grammatical subjects are consistent.** Again, look at the grammatical subjects of all your sentences. How many different subjects do you find? If you have too many different sentence subjects, your paragraph will be hard to follow. (Note: For the fun of it, underline the sentence subjects in the preceding paragraph. You'll find three, more or less: *you, the subject,* and *the reader.* The relationship among the three is what this paragraph is all about. Accordingly, the paragraph is coherent.)

> **Make sure your sentences look backward as well as forward.** In order for a paragraph to be coherent, each sentence should begin by linking itself firmly to the sentence that came before. If the link between sentences does not seem firm, use an introductory clause or phrase to connect one idea to the other.

> **Follow the principle of moving from old to new.** If you put the old information at the beginning of the sentence and the new information at the end, you accomplish two things: First, you ensure that your readers are on solid ground, moving from the familiar to the unknown. Second, because we tend to give emphasis to what comes at the end of a sentence, readers rightfully perceive that the new information is more important than the old.

> **Use repetition to create a sense of unity.** Repeating key words and phrases at appropriate moments will give your readers a sense of coherence in your work. But don't overdo it; you'll risk sounding redundant.

> **Use transition markers wisely.** Sometimes you'll need to announce to your readers a turn in your argument. Or you'll want to emphasize one point. Or you'll want to make clear a particular relationship in time. In all these cases you'll want to use transition markers. Here are some examples:
> * **To give an example:** *for example, for instance*
> * **To make a list:** *first, second, third, next, then*
> * **To show that you have more to say:** *in addition, furthermore, moreover*
> * **To indicate similarity:** *also, likewise, similarly*
> * **To show an exception:** *but, however, nevertheless, on the other hand*
> * **To show cause and effect:** *accordingly, consequently, therefore*

- **To emphasize:** *indeed, in fact, of course*
- **To conclude:** *finally, in conclusion, in the end*

Introductions and Conclusions Introductions and conclusions are among the most challenging of all paragraphs. Why? Because they must do more than simply state a topic sentence and offer support. Introductions and conclusions must synthesize and provide context for your entire argument, and they must also make the proper impression on your readers.

Introductions

The introduction is your chance to get readers interested in your subject. Accordingly, the tone of the paragraph has to be just right. You want to inform, but not to the point of being dull; you want to intrigue, but not to the point of being vague; you want to take a strong stance, but not to the point of alienating readers. Pay attention to the nuances of your tone. Seek out a second reader if you're not sure that you've managed to get the tone the way you want it.

Equally important to the tone of the introduction is that it needs to "place" your argument into a larger context. Here are some strategies:

> **Announce your topic broadly; then declare your particular take.** For example, if you're interested in talking about the symbolism of Fellini's films, you might (1) begin by saying that Fellini's symbolism has posed a problem for many of his critics, (2) provide a quick definition of the problem as others have defined it, and (3) declare your thesis (which states your own position on the matter).

> **Provide any background material important to your argument.** If you're interested in exploring how events in the 1960s influenced the work of Oliver Stone, in your introduction you'll want to provide the reader, in broad strokes, a description of the sixties. Don't include irrelevant details in your description; instead, emphasize those aspects of the culture (the assassination of John F. Kennedy, the war in Vietnam) that might have most influenced Stone.

> **Define key terms as you intend to make use of them in your argument.** If, for example, you're writing a paper on cinema verité, it is absolutely essential that you define the term for your reader. For example, how do you understand the term *verité*? How do you understand *reality*? Begin with a definition of terms, and from there work toward the declaration of your argument.

> **Use an anecdote or quotation.** Sometimes you'll find a terrific story or quotation that seems to reflect the main point of your paper. Don't be afraid to begin with it. Be sure, however, that you tie that story or quotation clearly and immediately to your main argument.

> **Acknowledge your opponents.** When you're writing a paper about a controversial matter, you might wish to begin by summarizing the point of view of your adversaries. Then state your own position in opposition to theirs. In this way you place yourself clearly in the ongoing conversation. Be careful, though; you don't want to make too convincing a case for the other side.

Remember, the introduction is the first impression that your argument will make on the reader. Take special care with your sentences so that they'll be interesting. Also take the time to consider who your readers are and what background they will bring with them to their reading. If your readers are very knowledgeable about the subject, you will not need to provide a lot of background information. If your readers are less knowledgeable, you will need to be more careful about defining terms.

Finally, you might want to consider writing the introduction *after* you've written the rest of the paper. Many writers find that they have a better grip on their subject once they've done a first draft. This "better grip" helps them to craft an introduction that is sure-footed, persuasive, interesting, and clear. (But be careful. Any changes that you make to an introduction and/or a thesis statement will affect the paper that follows. Simply adding the new introductory paragraph will not produce a "completed" paper.)

Conclusions

Conclusions are also difficult to write. How do you manage to make the reader feel persuaded by what you've said? Even if the points of your paper are strong, the overall effect of your argument might fall to pieces if the paper as a whole is badly concluded.

Many students end their papers by simply summarizing what has come before. A summary of what the reader has just read is important to the conclusion—particularly if your argument has been complicated or has covered a lot of ground. But a good conclusion will do more. Just as the introduction sought to place the paper in the larger, ongoing conversation about the topic, so should the conclusion insist on returning readers to that ongoing conversation, but with the feeling that they've learned something more. You don't want readers to finish your paper and say, "So what?" Admittedly, writing a conclusion isn't easy.

Many of the strategies we've listed for improving introductions can help you improve your conclusions as well. In the conclusion you might

> Return to the **ongoing conversation**, emphasizing the importance of your own contribution to it.

> Consider again the **background information** with which you began, and illustrate how your argument has shed new light on that information.

> Return to the **key terms** and point out how your essay has added new dimension to their meanings.

> Use an **anecdote or quotation** that summarizes or reflects your main idea.

> Acknowledge your **opponents**—if only to emphasize that you've beaten them.

> Remember, **language** is especially important to a conclusion. Your goal in the final sentences is to leave your ideas resounding in the reader's mind. Give the reader something to think about. Make your language ring.

Attending to Style

Most of us know good style when we see it. We also know when a sentence seems cumbersome to read. However, though we can easily spot beastly sentences, it is not as easy to say *why* a sentence—especially one that is grammatically correct—isn't working. We look at the sentence; we see that the commas are in the right places; we find no error to speak of. So why is the sentence so awful? What's gone wrong?

When thinking about what makes a good sentence, be sure to put yourself in the place of the reader. What is a reader hoping to find in your sentences? Information, yes. Eloquence, surely. But most importantly, a reader is looking for clarity. Your reader does not want to wrestle with sentences. She wants to read with ease. She wants to see one idea build on another. She wants to experience, without struggling, the emphasis of your language and the importance of your idea. Above all, she wants to feel that you, the writer, are doing the bulk of the work. In short, she wants to read sentences that are forceful, straightforward, and clear.[1]

Basic Principles of the Sentence
Focus on Actors and Actions

To understand what makes a good sentence, it's important to understand one principle: a sentence, at its very basic level, is about actors and actions. As such, the subject of a sentence should point clearly to the actor, and the verb of the sentence should describe the important action.

---

[1]The way of teaching writing style that is represented here has been greatly influenced by Joseph Williams and his work. For a thorough examination of the fundamental principles of style, see Williams's *Style: The Basics of Clarity and Grace*, 2nd ed. (New York: Pearson Longman, 2006).

This principle might seem so obvious to you that you don't think it warrants further discussion. But think again. Look at the following sentence, and then try to determine, in a nutshell, what's wrong with it:

> There is a question in the mind of some screenwriters over whether the employment of flashbacks is a sign of weakness in a script.

This sentence has no grammatical errors. But certainly it lumbers along, without any force.

Now consider the following sentence:

> Some screenwriters question whether flashbacks signify a weak script.

What changes does this sentence make? We can point to the more obvious changes: omitting the empty *there is* phrase; replacing the abstract noun *sign* with the stronger verb *signify*; replacing a second abstract noun *weakness* with the adjective *weak*; omitting all of the prepositions that the abstract nouns require. What principle governs these many changes? Precisely the one mentioned earlier: that the *actor* in a sentence should serve as the sentence's subject, and the *action* should be illustrated forcefully in the sentence's verbs.

Whenever you feel that your prose is confusing or hard to follow, find the actors and the actions of your sentences. Is the actor the subject of your sentence? Is the action related, vividly, in a verb? If not, rewrite your sentence accordingly.

Be Concrete

Student writers tend to rely too heavily on abstract nouns: they use *expectation* when the verb *expect* is stronger; they write *evaluation* when *evaluate* is more vivid. But why use an abstract noun when a verb will do better? Many students believe that abstract nouns permit them to sound more "academic." When you write with a lot of abstract nouns, however, you risk confusing your reader. You also end up cornering yourself syntactically. Consider the following:

> ❯ **Nouns often require prepositions.** Too many prepositional phrases in a sentence are hard to follow. Verbs, on the other hand, can stand on their own. They're cleaner; they don't box you in. If you need some proof of this claim, consider the following sentence:
>> An evaluation of the footage by the director is necessary prior to the cutting process.
>
> Notice all of the prepositional phrases that these nouns require. Now look at this sentence, which uses verbs:

> The director must evaluate the footage before cutting it.

This sentence has fewer nouns and prepositions, and is therefore much easier to read.

> **Abstract nouns often invite the *there is* construction.** Consider this sentence:

> There is a method of acting that Konstantin Stanislavsky invented in which acting students are taught about the use of past experiences to bring emotion to their roles.

We might rewrite this sentence as follows:

> Konstantin Stanislavsky invented a method that teaches actors to use past experiences to bring emotion to their roles.

The result, again, is a sentence that is more direct and easier to read.

> **Abstract nouns are, well, abstract.** Using too many abstract nouns will leave your prose seeming unrooted. Instead, use concrete nouns, as well as strong verbs, to convey your ideas.
> **Abstract nouns can obscure your logic.** Note how hard it is to follow the line of reasoning in the following sentence. (The nouns that might be rewritten as verbs or as adjectives are in boldface.)

> **Decisions** with regard to **the dismissal** of actors on the basis of **their unwillingness** to put on weight for a role rest with the director.

Now consider this sentence:

> When actors refuse to gain weight for a role, the director must decide whether or not to dismiss them.

The Exception: When to Use Abstract Nouns

In some instances an abstract noun will be essential to the sentence. Sometimes abstract nouns refer to a previous sentence (*these arguments, this decision,* etc.). Other times they allow you to be more concise (e.g., *her argument* versus *what she argued*). And in other cases, the abstract noun is a concept important to your argument: freedom, love, revolution, and so on. Still, if you examine your prose, you'll probably find that you overuse abstract nouns. Omitting from your writing those abstract nouns that aren't really necessary makes for leaner, "fitter" prose.

Be Concise

One of the most exasperating things about reading student texts is that most students don't know how to write concisely. Students use phrases when a single word will do. Or they offer pairs of adjectives and verbs where one is enough. Or they overwrite, saying the same thing two or three times with the hope that, one of those times, they'll get it the way they want it.

Stop the madness! It's easy to delete words and phrases from your prose once you've learned to be ruthless about it.

Do you really need words like *actually, basically, generally,* and so on? If you don't need them, why are they there? Are you using two words where one will do? Isn't *first and foremost* redundant? What's the point of *future* in *future plans*? And why do you keep saying, "In my opinion"? Doesn't the reader understand that this is *your* paper, based on *your* point of view?

Sometimes you won't be able to fix a wordy sentence by simply deleting a few words or phrases. You'll have to rewrite the whole sentence. Take the following sentence, for example:

> Plagiarism is a serious academic offense resulting in punishments that might include suspension or dismissal, profoundly affecting your academic career.

The idea here is simple: *Plagiarism is a serious offense with serious consequences.* Why not say so, simply?

Be Coherent

At this point in discussing style, we move from the sentence as a discrete unit to the way that sentences fit together. Coherence (or the lack of it) is a common problem in student papers. Sometimes a professor encounters a paper in which all the ideas seem to be there, but they're hard to follow. The prose seems jumbled. The line of reasoning is anything but linear. Couldn't the student have made this paper a bit more readable?

Although coherence is a complicated and difficult matter to address, we can offer a couple of tricks that will help your sentences "flow." Silly as it sounds, you should "dress" your sentences the way a bride might—wear, as the saying goes, something old and something new. In other words, each sentence you write should begin with the old—with something that looks back to the previous sentence. Then your sentence should move on to telling the reader something new. If you do this, your line of reasoning will be easier for readers to follow.

Though this advice sounds simple enough, it is not always easy to follow. Let's dissect the practice so that we can better understand how our sentences might be "well dressed."

Consider, first, the beginnings of sentences. The coherence of your paper depends largely on how well you begin sentences. "Well begun is half done." So says Mary Poppins, and in this case (as in all cases, really) she's right.

Beginning a sentence is hard work. When you begin a sentence, you have three important matters to consider:

1. **Is your topic also the subject of the sentence?** When a paper lacks coherence, usually it's because the writer has not been careful to ensure that the *topic* of the sentence is also the grammatical *subject* of the sentence. If, for instance, you're writing a sentence whose topic is the importance of the close-up in silent films, then the grammatical subject of the sentence should reflect that idea:

   > A silent-film actor's facial expressions were more important to his success than his body language was.

   If, on the other hand, you bury your topic in a subordinate clause, look what happens:

   > The rise of the silent-screen stars, which came about because of their faces, was not due to their control of body language.

   The emphasis and focus of the sentence are obscured.

2. **Are the topics/subjects of your sentences consistent?** For a paragraph to be coherent, most of the sentence subjects should be the same. To check for consistency, pick out a paragraph and make a list of its sentence subjects. See if any of the subjects seem out of place. For example, if you're writing a paragraph about the importance of the close-up in a paper on silent films, do most of your sentence subjects reflect that paragraph topic? Or do some of your sentences have "gestures" as the subject? Although the full-body comedy of silent-film stars like Charlie Chaplin and Buster Keaton may indeed have a place in your paper on silent films, you will confuse readers if your paragraph's sentence subjects point to too many competing ideas. Revise the sentences (perhaps the entire paragraph) for coherence.

3. **Have you marked, when appropriate, the transitions between ideas?** Coherence depends on how well you connect a sentence to the one that came before. You'll want to make solid transitions between your sentences, using words such as *however* or *therefore*. You'll also want to signal to readers whenever, for example, something important or disappointing comes up. In these cases, you'll want to use expressions such as *note that* or *unfortunately*. You might also want to indicate time or place in your argument. If so, you'll use transitions such as *then, later, earlier,* or *in the previous paragraph*. Be careful not to overuse transition phrases. Some writers think transition phrases can, all by themselves, direct a reader through an argument. Indeed, sometimes all a paragraph needs is a *however* in order for its argument suddenly to make sense. More often, though, the problem with coherence does not stem from a

lack of transition phrases, but from the fact that the writer has not articulated, for himself, the connections between his ideas. Don't rely on transition phrases alone to bring sense to muddled prose.

Be Emphatic

We've been talking about how sentences begin, but what about how they end?

If the beginnings of sentences must look over their shoulders at what came before, the ends of sentences must forge ahead into new ground. It's the end of a sentence, then, that must be courageous and emphatic. You must construct sentences so that the ends pack the punch.

To write emphatically, follow these principles:

> **As we've said, declare important ideas at the end of a sentence.** Shift less important ideas to the front.
> **Tighten the ends of sentences.** Don't trail off into nonsense, don't repeat yourself, and don't qualify what you've just said if you don't have to. Simply make your point and move on.
> **Use subordinate clauses to house subordinate ideas.** Put all the important ideas in main clauses and the less important ideas in subordinate clauses. If you have two ideas of equal importance that you want to express in the same sentence, use parallel constructions or semicolons. These two tricks of the trade are perhaps more useful than any others in balancing equally significant ideas.

Be in Control

When sentences run on and on, readers know that a writer has lost control. Take control of your sentences. When you read over your paper, look for sentences that never seem to end. Your first impulse might be to take these long sentences and divide them into two (or three or four). This simple solution often works. But sometimes this strategy isn't the most desirable one; it might lead to short, choppy sentences. Moreover, if you always cut your sentences in two, you'll never learn how a sentence can be long and complex without violating the boundaries of good prose.

What do you do when you encounter an overly long sentence? First consider the point of your sentence; usually it will have more than one point, and sorting out the points helps to sort out the grammar. Consider carefully the points that you're trying to make and the connections between those points. Then try to determine which grammatical structure best serves your purpose.

> **Are the points of equal importance?** Use a coordinating conjunction or a semicolon to join the ideas. Try to use parallel constructions when appropriate.

> **Are the points of unequal importance?** Use subordinate clauses or relative clauses to join the ideas.

> **Does one point make for an interesting aside?** Insert that point between commas, dashes, or even parentheses at the appropriate juncture in the sentence.

> **Do these ideas belong in the same sentence?** If not, create two sentences.

Write Beautifully

In your career as a writer you will sometimes produce a paper that is well written but could be written better. On this happy occasion, you might wish to turn your attention to such matters as balance, parallel structure, emphasis, rhythm, and word choice. If you're interested in exploring these rhetorical tools, you can consult one of several excellent style books, including Joe Williams's *Style: The Basics of Clarity and Grace*, Strunk and White's *The Elements of Style*, and John Trimble's *Writing With Style*. You will find valuable advice in these sources.

Revising: Cultivating a Critical Eye

Why and How to Revise

Most of us who compose on a computer understand revision as an ongoing, even constant process. Every time you hit the delete button, every time you cut and paste, every time you take out a comma or exchange one word for another, you're revising.

Real revision, however, is more than making a few changes here and there. Real revision requires that you open yourself up to the possibility that parts of your paper—even your entire paper—might need to be rethought, and rewritten.

Achieving this state of mind is difficult. First, you might be very attached to what you've written. You might be unwilling to change a word, let alone three or four paragraphs. Second, there's the matter of time: you might sense that the paper needs major work, but it's due tomorrow, or you have an exam in physics, or you're coming down with a cold and know that you need to sleep. Third, you might have difficulty understanding what, exactly, is wrong with your paper. Finally, you might simply be sick and tired of the paper. How can you make another pass through it when exhaustion has you in its grip? Why should you be bothered with (or overwhelmed by) the process of revising?

Of course, we might convince you that revision is worth the extra effort simply by saying that revising a paper will help you achieve a better grade. A good reader can sense when a piece of writing has been thoroughly considered and reconsidered. This *consideration* (and here we mean the word in both of its meanings) is not lost on your professor and will be rewarded.

More important than grades, however, is the fact that revising your papers teaches you to be a better writer. Studies have shown again and again that the best way to learn to write is to rewrite. In the revision process, you improve your reading skills and your analytical skills. You learn to challenge your own ideas, thus deepening and strengthening your argument. You learn to find the weaknesses in your writing. You may even discover patterns of error or habits of organization that are undermining your papers.

Though revising takes time and energy, it also helps you become a more efficient writer down the road. If, for example, you have discovered through the revision process that you tend to bury your topic sentences in the middle of the paragraph, you can take this discovery with you as you draft your next paper. You are less likely to make that particular mistake again.

Perhaps we've answered the question "Why should I revise?" The next question, of course, is "How?" There are many different kinds of revising:

> **Large-scale revision.** Large-scale revision means looking at the entire paper for places where your thinking seems to go awry. You might need to provide evidence, define terms, or add an entirely new step to your reasoning. You might even decide to restructure or rewrite your paper completely if you discover a new idea that intrigues you, or a structure that seems to be more effective than the one you've been using.

> **Small-scale revision.** Small-scale revision needs to happen when you know that a certain part of your paper isn't working. Maybe the introduction needs work. Maybe one part of the argument seems weak. Once you've located the problem, you'll focus on revising that one section of your paper. When you're finished you'll want to reconsider your paper as a whole to make sure that your revisions work in the context of the entire paper.

> **Editing.** Too often students confuse editing with revision. They are not the same processes. *Editing* is the process of finding minor problems with a text—problems that might easily be fixed by deleting a word or sentence, cutting and pasting a paragraph, and so on. When

you edit, you're considering your reader. *You* might be happy with how you've written your paper, but will your reader find your paper clear, readable, interesting? How can you rewrite the paper so that it's clearer, more concise, and, most important of all, a pleasure to read?

The very best writers revise their writing in all the ways listed here. To manage these various levels of revision, it's very important that you get an early start on your papers so that you have time to make any substantive, large-scale revisions that might be needed. Good writers also understand that revision is an ongoing process, not necessarily something that you do only after your first draft is complete. You might find, for example, that you're stuck halfway through the first draft of your paper. You decide to take a look at what you have so far. As you read, you find that you've neglected to make a point that is essential to the success of your argument. You revise what you've written, making that point clear. In the end, you find that your block is gone. Why? Maybe it's gone because what was blocking you in the first place was a hole in your argument. Or maybe it's gone because you gave your brain a break. In any case, stopping to revise in the middle of the drafting process often proves wise.

Developing Objectivity

We have yet to address the matter of how a writer knows what she should revise. Developing a critical eye is perhaps the most difficult part of the revision process. But having a critical eye makes you a better writer, reader, and thinker. So it's worth considering carefully how you might learn to see your own work with the objectivity that is essential to successful self-criticism.

The first step in gaining objectivity is to get some distance from your work. If you've planned your writing process well, you'll have left yourself a day or two to take a break. If you don't have this luxury, even an hour of video games or a walk over to the printing center to pick up a hard copy of your draft might be enough to clear your head. Many writers find that their mind keeps working on their papers even while their attention is turned elsewhere. When they return to their work, they bring with them a fresh perspective. They also bring a more open, more detached mind.

When you return to your paper, the first thing that you'll want to do is consider whether or not the paper as a whole meets your (and your professor's) expectations. Read the paper through without stopping (don't get hung up on one troublesome paragraph). Then ask yourself these questions:

> **Did I fulfill the assignment?** If the professor gave you instructions for this assignment, reread them and then ask yourself whether or

not you've addressed all of the matters you're expected to address. Does your paper stray from the assignment? If it does, have you worked to make your argument relevant, or are you coming out of left field? If the professor hasn't given you explicit instructions for this paper, you'll still want to take a moment to consider what the professor expects. What books has the professor asked you to read? What position do they take toward your topic? Has the professor emphasized a certain method of scholarship (feminism, Marxism, etc.)? Has he said anything to you about research methods in his discipline? Does your paper seem to fit into the conversation that the professor has been carrying on in class? Have you written something that other students would find relevant and interesting?

> **Did I say what I intended to say?** This is perhaps the most difficult question you will ask yourself in the revision process. Many of us think that we have indeed said what we intended to say. When we read our papers, we're able to fill in any holes that might exist in our arguments with the information that we have in our minds. The problem is that our readers sometimes don't have this information in mind. They fall into the holes of our arguments and can't get out. It's very important, therefore, to think carefully about what you've said—and to think just as carefully about what you haven't said. Ask yourself these questions: Was I clear? Do I need to define my terms? Has every stage of the argument been articulated clearly? Have I made adequate transitions between my ideas? Is my logic solid? Is it *there*, for all to see? If the answer to any of these questions is no, you will want to revise your draft.

> **What are the strengths of my paper?** In order to develop a critical eye, it's just as important to know when you've written well as it is to know when you've written poorly. It helps, therefore, to make a list of what you think you've done well in your draft. It's also helpful to pick out your favorite or strongest paragraph. When you find a good paragraph, sentence, or idea, think about why it's good. You'll not only be gaining an understanding of what it means to write well, but you'll also be giving yourself a pat on the back—something that's very important to do in the revision process.

> **What are the weaknesses of my paper?** Looking for weaknesses isn't as fun as looking for strengths, but it's necessary to the revision process. Again, try to make a list of what you haven't done well in this paper. Your list should be as specific as you can make it. Instead of writing, "Problems with paragraphs" you might say, "Problems with unity in my paragraphs," or even more specific, "Problems with the transitions

between paragraphs 3 and 4, and 12 and 13." Also force yourself to
determine which paragraph (or sentence) you like least in the paper.
Figure out why you don't like it, and work to make it better. Then go
back through your paper and look for others like it.

Analyzing Your Work

If you've been considering the strengths and weaknesses of your paper,
you've already begun to analyze your work. The process of analysis involves
breaking down an idea or an argument into its parts and evaluating those
parts on their merits. When you analyze your own paper, then, you're breaking down that paper into its parts and asking yourself whether or not these
parts support the paper as you envision it.

The following checklist reiterates our earlier advice. Use it to analyze
your whole paper, or use it to help you figure out what has gone wrong with
a particular part of your work.

> **Consider your introduction**
>   - If you're writing a research paper, does the introduction place your
>   argument in an ongoing conversation?
>   - If you're not writing a research paper, does the introduction
>   establish context?
>   - Does the introduction define all of your key terms?
>   - Does the introduction draw the reader in?
>   - Does the introduction lead the reader clearly to your thesis?
> **Consider your thesis**
>   - Does the thesis say what you want it to say?
>   - Does the thesis make a point worth considering? Does it answer the
>   question, "So what?"
>   - Does the thesis provide the reader with some sense of the paper's
>   structure?
>   - Does the paper deliver what your thesis promises to deliver?
> **Consider your structure**
>   - Make an outline of the paper you've just written. Does this outline
>   reflect your intentions?
>   - Does this outline make sense, or are there gaps in the logic—places
>   where you've asked your readers to make leaps for which they
>   haven't been prepared?
>   - Is each point in the outline adequately developed?
>   - Is each point equally developed? (That is, does your paper seem
>   balanced overall?)

- Is each point relevant? Interesting?
- Underline the thesis sentence and all of the topic sentences. Then cut and paste them together to form a paragraph. Does this paragraph make sense?

> **Consider your paragraphs**

- Does each paragraph have a topic sentence that clearly controls it?
- Are the paragraphs internally coherent?
- Are the paragraphs externally coherent? (That is, have you made adequate transitions between paragraphs? Is each paragraph clearly related to the thesis?)

> **Consider your argument and its logic**

- Have you really presented an argument, or is your paper merely a series of observations, a summary?
- Do you see any holes in your argument, or do you find it convincing?
- Have you dealt fairly with the opposition? Or have you neglected to mention other possible arguments concerning your topic for fear that they might undermine your work?
- Have you supplied ample evidence for your arguments?

> **Consider your conclusion**

- Is the conclusion appropriate, or does it introduce a completely new idea?
- Does the conclusion sum up the main point of the paper?
- Does the conclusion leave the reader with something to think about?
- Does the language resonate, or does it fall flat? Have you inflated the language ridiculously to try to pad a conclusion that is empty and ineffective?

Proofreading and Formatting

The final step that you'll want to take before submitting your paper is to make sure that the grammar, spelling, and punctuation throughout the paper are correct and that you've formatted it appropriately. These details may seem frustratingly minor, but errors often cause readers to grow impatient with otherwise well-written essays. So be sure to take the time to carefully *proofread* your essay.

When you proofread, you need to slow down your reading, allowing your eye to focus on every word, every phrase of your paper. Reading aloud can help you slow down, pointing your attention to errors that have gone unseen. Look for common errors—like pronoun agreement, spelling errors, subject–verb agreement, *its/it's* confusion, *their/there* confusion, and so on— as you read. If you have time, get the opinion of a second reader. Treat the proofreading stage as you would a word search or sudoku puzzle—as a puzzle to be solved. No doubt, some errors are lurking in your prose (even professional writers find errors when they proofread their own work). It should be your mission to find them and root them out.

You'll also want to format the paper correctly. Some instructors provide explicit directions about constructing a title page, choosing a font, setting margins, paginating, footnoting, and so on. Be sure to follow these instructions carefully. If the instructor does not provide directions, consult the *MLA* (Modern Language Association) *Handbook*—the standard reference for writers in the humanities—for specific advice. Instructors appreciate papers that are not only well written, but also beautifully presented.